Customer Service
Excellence
Clear Communication for Optimal Outcomes

Table of Contents

1. Introduction 1

2. Understanding the Vital Role of Communication in Customer
Service 2

    2.1. The Essence of Customer Service Communication 2

    2.2. The Impact of Effective Communication on Customer
Satisfaction 3

    2.3. The Role of Active Listening in Customer Service 3

    2.4. Strategies for Enhancing Communication in Customer
Service 4

3. Unmasking the Key Elements of Excellent Customer Service 6

    3.1. Essential Element 1: Empathy 6

    3.2. Essential Element 2: Responsiveness 6

    3.3. Essential Element 3: Knowledge 7

    3.4. Essential Element 4: Communication Skills 7

    3.5. Essential Element 5: Problem-Solving Skills 7

    3.6. Essential Element 6: Adaptability 8

    3.7. Essential Element 7: Composure 8

    3.8. Essential Element 8: Consistency 8

    3.9. Essential Element 9: Follow-through 9

4. The Art and Science of Active Listening 10

    4.1. The Anatomy of Active Listening 10

5. Understanding 11

6. Acknowledgment 12

7. Thoughtful Response 13

    7.1. Mastering the Techniques of Active Listening 13

8. Focus 14

9. Paraphrasing and Summarising 15

10. Asking Probing Questions 16

11. Providing Feedback 17

    11.1. Importance of Emotional Intelligence in Active Listening .. 17

12. Self-Awareness 18

13. Empathy 19

    13.1. Challenges in Active Listening and Overcoming Them 19

14. Prejudices and Preconceptions 20

15. Assumptions 21

16. Distractions 22

    16.1. Conclusion 22

17. Mastering the Power of Non-Verbal Communication in
Customer Interactions 23

    17.1. Understanding the Basics of Non-Verbal Communication .. 23

    17.2. Decoding Facial Expressions 23

    17.3. Sound of Silence: Understanding Pauses and Silence 24

    17.4. Interpreting Voice Tone, Pitch, and Pace 24

    17.5. Power of Body Language 24

    17.6. The Role of Eye Contact 25

    17.7. Interpreting the Use of Space 25

    17.8. Non-Verbal Communication in Digital Interactions 25

    17.9. Empathy is the Key 25

    17.10. Practice Makes Perfect 25

18. Emotional Intelligence: The Untold Secret to Customer
Satisfaction 27

    18.1. Understanding Emotional Intelligence 27

    18.2. Emotional Intelligence: The Anatomy 28

    18.3. Cultivating Emotional Intelligence 29

    18.4. Emotional Intelligence in Action 30

    18.5. Conclusion 30

19. Overcoming Communication Barriers for a Seamless
Customer Experience 32

19.1. Identifying Communication Barriers 32

19.2. Language and Cultural Differences 32

19.3. Inconsistent Messaging 33

19.4. Lack of Clarity 33

19.5. Poor Listening Skills 34

19.6. Leveraging Technology in Breaking Communication
Barriers 34

19.7. Nurturing a Communication-Centric Culture 35

19.8. Conclusion: Towards a Seamless Customer Experience 35

20. Strategies for Dealing with Difficult Customers and Managing
Conflicts 36

20.1. Identifying Difficult Customers 36

20.2. Root Causes of Difficulty 36

20.3. Patience is a Virtue 37

20.4. Active Listening 37

20.5. Appropriate Problem Solving 37

20.6. Conflict Management Techniques 37

20.7. When to Escalate and When to Let Go 38

20.8. Training and Support for Staff 38

20.9. Learn and Improve 38

21. Advancing from Customer Satisfaction to Customer Delight 39

21.1. Understanding Customer Delight 39

21.2. The Shift from Satisfaction to Delight 40

21.3. Creating a Culture of Customer Delight 40

21.4. Leveraging Technology for Delight 41

21.5. Measuring Customer Delight 41

21.6. Piloting Challenges 42

22. Leveraging Technology for Enhanced Customer
Communications 43

22.1. Understanding Your Customer Communication Channels . . 43

22.2. Harnessing the Power of Social Media 44

22.3. Integrating Live Chat and Chatbots 44

22.4. Efficient Email Automation 45

22.5. Leveraging CRM Tools 45

22.6. Implementing Self-Service Options 45

22.7. Harnessing Big Data for Customer Insights 46

23. Measuring Outcomes: Tools to Assess and Improve Customer

Service Excellence 47

23.1. Understanding the Need for Measuring Outcomes 47

23.2. Quantitative Tools 47

23.3. Qualitative Tools 48

23.4. Leveraging Technological Tools 49

23.5. Combining Tools for Comprehensive Metrics 49

Chapter 1. Introduction

Welcome to an illuminating exploration of "Customer Service Excellence: Clear Communication for Optimal Outcomes!" This Special Report has been meticulously crafted to ensure your journey towards impeccable customer service is not only informative but also engaging. Inside, you'll find perspicuous language, real-world examples, and easy-to-understand strategies that cut through technical jargon and empower you to establish an unparalleled rapport with your customers. Outstanding customer service is no longer just a desirable part of business: it's a critical one, and this report serves as your key to unlocking that potential. Get ready to revolutionize your approach to customer interactions, promoting clear communication, increasing satisfaction, and propelling your business growth to the stratosphere. So, gear up! Your journey towards cultivating an environment of customer service excellence starts here!

Chapter 2. Understanding the Vital Role of Communication in Customer Service

Communication is often said to be at the heart of good customer service. It's through effective communication that companies lead their customers from initial engagement to continued loyalty, ensuring satisfaction at every stage of the process. But why does communication matter so much in customer service, and how can it be improved to deliver optimal results?

2.1. The Essence of Customer Service Communication

Customer service communication encompasses a wide range of activities, from answering simple queries to resolving complex complaints, advising on product selection, and maintaining ongoing dialogue with customers. These activities are often facilitated by various means, including face-to-face interactions, phone calls, emails, social media, and more.

What ties all these activities together is the use of communication. For instance, a customer service representative needs to understand a customer's needs, which can only be identified through communication. Likewise, the representative needs to convey information or tools for the customer's use, again, it's only possible through communication.

Despite this wide range of tasks and methods, the essence of customer service communication remains the same: to create a productive and positive experience for the customer, building trust and satisfaction throughout each interaction.

2.2. The Impact of Effective Communication on Customer Satisfaction

Effective communication can significantly enhance customer satisfaction. This correlation stems from the ability of good communication to clarify misunderstandings, educate customers about products or services, solve problems swiftly, and make customers feel heard and valued.

When customer service representatives communicate effectively, they can understand the needs and expectations of customers better. This understanding, in turn, allows them to provide solutions and suggestions tailored to the customer, significantly improving their overall satisfaction with the service they receive.

Equally, good communication helps representatives to inform the customer about the processes involved in their request or complaint. This can lead to realistic expectations, further enhancing satisfaction as customers understand the reasoning behind a decision or delay.

2.3. The Role of Active Listening in Customer Service

Active listening is a vital communication skill in customer service. It involves fully focusing on the speaker, avoiding distractions, demonstrating that you are listening (for example, through non-verbal cues or paraphrasing), and providing valuable feedback that is relevant to what's being said.

Active listening also entails demonstrating empathy – an understanding and sharing of the feelings of another. In a customer service setting, empathy can significantly influence the outcome of an interaction, as it can help de-escalate emotions and make the customer feel seen, heard, and understood.

Active listening not only helps to identify problems more accurately and provide appropriate solutions but also ensures that the customer feels valued and respected. This can lead to increased customer loyalty and, in turn, higher retention rates.

2.4. Strategies for Enhancing Communication in Customer Service

Good communication in customer service does not happen by chance. It requires intentional strategies and deliberate effort. Here are key strategies to consider:

1. **Training:** Skill-building programs can help customer service representatives improve their communication skills, covering everything from active listening to empathy, clarity, conciseness, and more.

2. **Feedback:** Regular evaluations and constructive feedback give representatives a clear idea of their strengths and areas for improvement. Through feedback, they can continuously refine their communication skills to better meet customer needs.

3. **Embrace Technology:** Various technologies can aid in improving communication, including CRM systems, live chat support, speech analytics, and more. These tools can improve response times, personalization of messages, and overall communication efficiency.

4. **Creating a Customer-Centric Culture:** Creating a culture that values the customer has an indirect but significant effect on communication. When representatives know that the customer is at the center of the organization's activities, they are likely to

4

prioritize clear, respectful, and proactive communication.

In conclusion, communication plays an integral role in customer service, influencing every aspect of interactions with customers. By understanding its importance and improving its effectiveness, customer service teams can create more satisfying experiences for customers, thereby fostering loyalty and driving substantial business growth. With the right strategies and tools in place, organizations can transform their customer service communication and realize their full potential in an increasingly competitive business landscape.

Remember, mastering customer service communication is not an overnight job. It's an ongoing process of learning, practice, and refinement. Every interaction offers an opportunity to learn more about your customers, hone your communication skills, and contribute to an enhanced customer service experience.

Take the step today to amplify your communication skills; your customers, and indeed your entire organization, stand to benefit from this noble endeavor.

Chapter 3. Unmasking the Key Elements of Excellent Customer Service

To provide excellent customer service, one must understand its essential elements. These elements, when put into practice, lead to customer satisfaction, loyalty, and therefore increased profitability.

3.1. Essential Element 1: Empathy

Empathy is critical to customer service excellence. It involves understanding and sharing another person's feelings, essentially putting yourself in their shoes. In customer service, empathy means understanding the customer's needs, frustrations, and desires.

When customer service representatives show genuine empathy, customers feel understood and valued. This can be demonstrated by listening carefully, acknowledging the customer's feelings, and expressing understanding verbally.

3.2. Essential Element 2: Responsiveness

Customers appreciate quick responses to their inquiries, complaints, or issues. They like to feel that their time is respected. Improving response times can significantly boost customer satisfaction.

Techniques to increase responsiveness include setting realistic expectations, deploying live chat functionality, ensuring that there is enough customer service support, and streamlining customer service processes.

3.3. Essential Element 3: Knowledge

A knowledgeable customer service representative answers questions accurately and quickly. The representative should have an extensive understanding of the company's products or services, policies, and procedures.

Proper training and providing accessible information resources to customer service staff can improve their knowledge and confidence. This will result in quicker, more accurate responses.

3.4. Essential Element 4: Communication Skills

Clear, concise, and polite communication is fundamental to excellent customer service. Good communication skills entail listening effectively, explaining things clearly, and being respectful in all interactions.

Meeting this element involves training staff in effective communication methods, including verbal and non-verbal cues, email etiquette, and proper language use.

3.5. Essential Element 5: Problem-Solving Skills

Customers usually contact customer service to solve a problem. Hence, problem-solving is a key skill for customer service representatives. This includes understanding the issue, finding viable solutions, and implementing those solutions effectively.

Developing this skill involves analytical thinking, creativity, and occasionally, a willingness to bend the rules. Companies can develop this skill in their staff through training, workshops, and practical problem-solving exercises.

3.6. Essential Element 6: Adaptability

Every customer is unique, as is every problem or query. Thus, customer service personnel need to be adaptable and flexible. They need to adjust their approach according to the customer's needs, personality, or the nature of their issue.

To equip staff in adapting to varying customer needs, companies can employ role-playing exercises, real-world case studies, and provide decision-making autonomy to their representatives.

3.7. Essential Element 7: Composure

In the face of an unhappy customer or a complicated problem, remaining composed is vital. A calm, patient, and composed representative helps to defuse tension and makes the customer feel at ease.

To nurture this attribute, companies can provide stress management training, foster a supportive work environment, and encourage regular breaks to maintain mental freshness and prevent burnout.

3.8. Essential Element 8: Consistency

Consistency in delivering high-quality service is crucial for maintaining customer satisfaction. Customers like to know what to expect when they contact customer service. They want the same level of care, respect, and quality service each time.

Strategies for maintaining consistency include setting standard procedures, regular staff training and evaluation, and utilizing quality assurance measures.

3.9. Essential Element 9: Follow-through

When a representative assures a customer that they will do something - such as calling them back or escalating their issue - the customer expects them to follow through. Not doing so damages trust.

You can better ensure follow-through by implementing tracking systems for customer inquiries or complaints, and setting up accountability measures for your customer service personnel.

In conclusion, understanding and implementing these nine key elements can significantly improve a company's customer service quality, thereby enhancing customer satisfaction and growing profitability. By doing so, you will not only meet the basic requirements of your customers but exceed their expectations, fostering long-term loyalty and investment in your brand.

Chapter 4. The Art and Science of Active Listening

Active listening lies at the heart of any meaningful interaction, more so in the realm of customer service where clear understanding forms the backbone to optimal outcomes. A powerful skill, active listening enables you to fully comprehend the customer's concerns, validate their feelings, and arrive at solutions that align with their needs.

4.1. The Anatomy of Active Listening

Before we delve into the mechanics and techniques of active listening, let's explore what it means. Active listening goes beyond merely hearing words; it implies understanding the message, acknowledging the speaker's perspective, and responding thoughtfully.

Chapter 5. Understanding

To fully grasp the speaker's message, it's essential to listen beyond just the words they're saying. Their tone of voice, pace and pauses, body language, and even what they're not saying can all deliver significant context. When dealing with customers, look out for subtle hints of dissatisfaction, impatience or confusion, then responding accordingly.

Chapter 6. Acknowledgment

Acknowledgment validates the customer's perspective, building trust and rapport. A simple nod or a verbal affirmation like, "I can understand..." or "It must have been difficult..." can go a long way in fostering a positive conversation. Keep in mind, acknowledging is not necessarily agreeing, but rather demonstrating that the speaker's feelings and perceptions are important and valid.

Chapter 7. Thoughtful Response

The final part of active listening is the response, which should be mindful, deliberate, and relevant. This means appropriately addressing all points mentioned, summarising the main elements, and identifying any next steps.

7.1. Mastering the Techniques of Active Listening

Now that we understand the components of active listening, let's examine the techniques that can help us become expert active listeners in customer service.

Chapter 8. Focus

Distractions are detrimental to active listening. During a conversation with a customer, give your complete attention to them. Ignore distractors such as background noise, mobile phones, emails, or other tasks. Ensure your body language communicates attentiveness; maintain eye contact when face-to-face, or modulate your tone to reflect interest if you're on a call.

Chapter 9. Paraphrasing and Summarising

Rewording the customer's statements not only ensures your understanding but also reassures them that you're attentive. Summarisation, on the other hand, involves presenting the main points at various intervals or at the end of the conversation. It's a powerful way to consolidate understanding and establish agreement on the issues at hand.

Chapter 10. Asking Probing Questions

Asking questions serves dual purposes: understanding the issue better and exhibiting interest. Use predominantly open-ended questions – those that cannot be answered with a simple 'yes' or 'no' – to encourage more explanation and facilitate a deeper understanding.

Chapter 11. Providing Feedback

Providing feedback involves sharing your understanding, offering opportunities for clarification, or introducing new perspectives. Remember, feedback is not about correcting or disagreeing, it's about seeking clarity and ensuring the message is understood precisely.

11.1. Importance of Emotional Intelligence in Active Listening

Emotional intelligence, or EQ, refers to the ability to understand, manage, and use our emotions in positive ways. Integrating emotional intelligence into active listening equips you with a better understanding of the emotional nuances in the customer's dialogue, leading to a more informed and empathetic response.

Chapter 12. Self-Awareness

Being aware of your own emotional state is crucial. It prevents unnecessary emotional reactions on your part and enables management of any biases or mental filters that might interfere with understanding.

Chapter 13. Empathy

Genuine empathy builds trust and rapport, and it makes the customer feel valued. Place yourself in the customer's shoes to gain an understanding of their perspective, feelings, and challenges.

13.1. Challenges in Active Listening and Overcoming Them

Despite its importance, several barriers can hinder active listening. However, being aware of these can help us counteract them effectively.

Chapter 14. Prejudices and Preconceptions

Allowing preconceptions or prejudices to influence your understanding can create communication gaps. Treat each conversation as an opportunity to learn about the customer's unique experience and perspective.

Chapter 15. Assumptions

Assumption is the enemy of active listening. They obscure the real message and can lead to miscommunication. Therefore, verify before you conclude to ensure accurate comprehension.

Chapter 16. Distractions

Physical, digital, and mental distractions inhibit active listening. Creating a conducive environment for communication, keeping a clear mind, and prioritizing the conversation can counteract these.

16.1. Conclusion

Mastering the art and science of active listening can transform your customer service experience. While it requires patience, practice, and empathy, cultivating this skill results in satisfied customers, resolved problems, and enhanced customer loyalty. Always remember, in the realm of customer service, the sound of listening is often louder than words.

Chapter 17. Mastering the Power of Non-Verbal Communication in Customer Interactions

Sometimes words aren't enough. When dealing with customers, knowing what isn't being said is often just as essential as understanding the words themselves. This insight takes us to non-verbal communication, a powerful tool in shaping customer experiences.

17.1. Understanding the Basics of Non-Verbal Communication

Non-verbal communication is a broad term encompassing many different forms of unspoken interaction. It includes elements like body language, tone of voice, facial expressions, eye contact, physical distance, and others. Daniel Goleman likens non-verbal signals to a "second conversation," one that takes place alongside spoken communication. It's critical to be fluent in this second conversation to fully comprehend what a customer wishes to communicate.

17.2. Decoding Facial Expressions

Facial expressions transmit a wealth of information. Researchers argue that at least seven emotions are universally expressed and recognized through facial expressions: happiness, sadness, anger, surprise, fear, disgust, and contempt. By understanding these basic expressions, we can better respond to customers' needs, even when they haven't been verbalized.

A satisfied smile on a customer's face solidifies that they're pleased with the service. Conversely, a frown or scowl can suggest dissatisfaction or confusion.

17.3. Sound of Silence: Understanding Pauses and Silence

Silences in conversation often hold valuable information. Long pauses could indicate doubt, hesitation, or a customer's need for more time to make a decision. In these situations, resist the urge to fill the silence. Instead, let the customer dictate the pace of the conversation.

17.4. Interpreting Voice Tone, Pitch, and Pace

Voice characteristics can reveal how a customer feels about the conversation. A rapid speech pace might mean excitement or nervousness, while a slow pace suggests the customer is thinking carefully about his or her words. Paying attention to the tone and pitch can help to gauge the customer's comfort level and emotions accurately.

17.5. Power of Body Language

Body language is another crucial aspect of non-verbal communication. Open body language, such as uncrossed arms and leaning towards the speaker, often suggests receptiveness. On the other hand, crossed arms, lack of eye contact, or turning away may indicate discomfort or disinterest.

17.6. The Role of Eye Contact

Maintaining an appropriate level of eye contact displays attentiveness and interest in what the customer is saying. It's an essential aspect of building trust with your customer, making them feel important and validated.

17.7. Interpreting the Use of Space

Personal space varies greatly from culture to culture. Understanding and respecting a customer's personal space can significantly impact their comfort and satisfaction.

17.8. Non-Verbal Communication in Digital Interactions

In today's digital era, non-verbal communication extends to online interactions as well. Paying attention to the timing, responsiveness, and tone of written communications can provide valuable insights into a customer's sentiments.

17.9. Empathy is the Key

Empathy is the anchor of effective non-verbal communication. It allows you to comprehend the feelings of customers better by "feeling with" them. This can guide your responses and interactions, leading to improved satisfaction and trust.

17.10. Practice Makes Perfect

The art of non-verbal communication is a gained skill, which requires continuous practice and refinement. Implementing role-plays, training sessions, and providing regular feedback can help customer service teams master these non-verbal cues for more meaningful interactions.

Understanding and tapping into non-verbal communication can significantly elevate a company's customer service approach. It grants a deeper understanding of customer needs and feelings, leading to better relationships, increased satisfaction, and ultimately, a stronger brand reputation. So, approach customer interactions with an open mind and an open heart. Your attention to non-verbal cues will foster an environment of trust, empathy, and service.

Chapter 18. Emotional Intelligence: The Untold Secret to Customer Satisfaction

The irrefutable power of emotional intelligence in a customer service setting lies in its astonishing ability to create connections, engender loyalty, and resolve conflicts with unruly clients. It's the bridge that spans the chasm between dry business transactions and deeply personalized customer experiences.

18.1. Understanding Emotional Intelligence

Emotional intelligence (EI) refers to the capacity for recognizing our own feelings and those of others, for motivating ourselves, and for managing emotions effectively in ourselves and others. An emotionally intelligent individual is both highly conscious of their own emotional states, even negativity—frustration, sadness, or something more subtle, and able to identify and manage them. These are key factors in personal success and mental well-being.

In the realm of customer service, where communication, empathy, and interpersonal relations are pivotal, EI becomes particularly relevant. It allows professionals to navigate though emotional undercurrents, recognize customers' needs beneath the surface, and respond effectively. A high level of EI in customer service staff equates the ability to handle difficult interactions, build strong customer relationships, and foster a positive environment.

18.2. Emotional Intelligence: The Anatomy

Broadly speaking, EI consists of four major components:

1. Self-awareness

2. Self-management

3. Social awareness

4. Relationship management

Each of these aspects plays a key role in delivering exceptional customer service.

Self-awareness is about recognizing and understanding your own emotions. This dimension of EI allows you to tune into your feelings, trust your instincts, and make decisions that align with your core values. In a customer service context, self-awareness aids representatives in identifying their emotional triggers and preemptively managing reactions.

Self-management, on the other hand, deals with your ability to control and manage your emotional reactions. It involves being responsible for your own behavior, especially in stressful or difficult situations. Self-management can be a deciding factor between a heated argument and a constructive conversation with a customer.

Social awareness refers to the talent for understanding other people's emotions, needs, and concerns. It's about being able to pick up on emotional cues, listen actively, and respond appropriately. In customer service, social awareness can mean the difference between dismissing a customer's issues and making them feel understood and valued.

Relationship management revolves around skillfully handling and influencing other people's emotions. It's essentially about leveraging your control over your emotions and your understanding of others' feelings to manage interactions successfully. In a customer service setting, this could translate into resolving conflicts, dispelling customer dissatisfaction, or turning around a negative customer experience.

18.3. Cultivating Emotional Intelligence

Improving your EI encompasses enhancing skills linked to its four components. Here are some strategies you can employ:

To **boost self-awareness**, make regular self-reflection a habit. Take note of your emotional responses to different situations and what triggers them. Recognizing these patterns is the first step towards mastering your emotions.

To **enhance self-management**, learn to take a pause. While in a tricky conversation with a customer, instead of reacting instantly, take a moment. Breathe in, compose yourself, think, and then respond. This delay, however trivial it may seem, provides an opportunity for better response management.

To **develop social awareness**, practice active listening. Ensure to fully understand the customers' point of view before responding. This strategy not only makes them feel valued but can also provide valuable insight into their concerns or needs.

To **better relationship management**, consider the emotions of the customer in your responses. Acknowledging the customer's feelings and empathizing can often deescalate fraught situations.

18.4. Emotional Intelligence in Action

Incorporating EI in your customer service approach can transform interactions. Assume you're faced with a disgruntled customer who's upset with a faulty product.

Upon encountering the situation, a representative with a high level of self-awareness would recognize any frustration triggered by the customer's harsh words. They'd use their self-management skills to suppress any defensive reactions, maintaining a calm demeanor instead.

Having tuned into their feelings, the representative can now focus on the client, indicating social awareness. Through active listening, they'll pick up on the customer's disappointment and perhaps a sense of betrayal. They can acknowledge these feelings, empathizing with the customer's unfortunate experience.

Next, the representative can use relationship management skills to navigate the conversation towards a resolution. They could offer a genuine apology, propose a replacement or a refund, and reassure the customer of better product quality in the future. Despite the customer's initial anger, an emotionally intelligent approach not only resolves the conflict but potentially converts an unhappy customer into a brand advocate.

18.5. Conclusion

Possessing emotional intelligence isn't about achieving perfection. It's about broadening your capacity to resonate with others, offering help, support, or solution from a place of genuine understanding. In customer service, where every interaction matters, integrating EI into your strategies can lead to happier customers, a more harmonious work environment, and ultimately, a thriving business.

Remember, people may not remember exactly what you did or what you said, but they will always remember how you made them feel.

Chapter 19. Overcoming Communication Barriers for a Seamless Customer Experience

Effective customer service hinges on a solid framework of unhindered communication. While the complexity of interactions may vary from one customer to the next, the essence of delivering a seamless customer experience always boils down to breaking through the barriers of communication — of truly hearing and empathizing with the needs of your customers. This journey of ours will illuminate key components on how you can achieve this.

19.1. Identifying Communication Barriers

The initial steps to overcoming barriers in communication are identifying and understanding them. Communication barriers may exist in various forms, including language and cultural differences, inconsistent messaging, a lack of clarity, and the inability to listen effectively. Being able to spot these barriers is a stepping stone to developing strategies to overcome them in the pursuit of providing an unparalleled customer experience.

19.2. Language and Cultural Differences

In an increasingly globalized world, language and cultural differences pose significant challenges in communication. This becomes particularly salient in customer service, where clear comprehension is key. The use of colloquialisms, jargon, or acronyms that a customer may not comprehend can sever the lines of communication.

To overcome this, your approach should be to encourage language sensitivity. Adopt simple and universally understood terminology. Embrace the diversity in culture and language to enhance your customer interactions. Training can be provided to customer service representatives to enhance their cultural competence and language proficiency.

19.3. Inconsistent Messaging

The inconsistent messaging can create confusion, leading to a disjointed customer experience. When interactions with different departments deliver varying information, customers can become frustrated, causing an erosion of trust.

One approach to ensure consistent messaging is to employ a robust internal communication system. Establish a common platform where information, updates, and changes can be quickly disseminated throughout the team. Having a unified voice in your organization is crucial to maintain consistency in your interactions.

19.4. Lack of Clarity

Communicating with customers demands precision and clarity. Anything less can result in misunderstandings and, ultimately, unsatisfied customers. To overcome issues related to a lack of clarity, be direct and concise in your communication. Avoid ambiguity and unnecessary complexities. Use easily understandable language and concepts, and make sure your customer comprehends the information by asking clarifying questions.

19.5. Poor Listening Skills

In the realm of customer service, listening is just as important as speaking. It's not just about having conversations with customers, it's about understanding their needs, concerns, and expectations. Effective listening can foster a sense of empathy, enabling representatives to personalize their responses, leading to increased customer satisfaction.

To improve listening skills within your customer service team, enforce training that emphasizes active listening. Allow your customers to express their thoughts without interruption, demonstrate understanding through nodding or paraphrasing, and respond appropriately.

19.6. Leveraging Technology in Breaking Communication Barriers

With the advent of digital technology, the nature of customer service has evolved. The digital age presents new opportunities as well as challenges, particularly in the field of communication. The key lies in striking a balance between embracing technology and fostering genuine human connection.

One way to leverage technology is through the deployment of AI-powered chatbots, which can provide instantaneous, 24/7 customer support. However, ensure that the option for communicating with a real human representative is always available. Automated processes cannot replace the compassion and understanding that humans bring.

19.7. Nurturing a Communication-Centric Culture

Culture plays a significant role in shaping behavior and attitudes within an organization. By fostering a culture that values open and clear communication, the principles can be engrained into the work ethic of every team member.

One way to achieve this is by modeling good communication behavior from the top and encouraging consistent practice across all levels of the organization. Regularly recognizing and rewarding good communication can also incentivize its practice.

19.8. Conclusion: Towards a Seamless Customer Experience

Overcoming communication barriers for a seamless customer experience doesn't occur overnight. It requires consistent effort, training, and a willingness to continually learn and evolve. Ensuring the wheels of communication are turning smoothly and effectively is integral to delivering excellent customer service. By identifying and diligently working to overcome these barriers, you are unlocking the gateway to impeccable customer service and outstanding business growth.

This journey might be challenging, but the improvement in customer satisfaction and the potential business growth that it can yield makes it a worthwhile expedition. Your journey towards creating that seamless synergy between your organization and your customers is a continuous one, but remember that every step taken towards enhancing your communication is a leap towards achieving customer service excellence.

Chapter 20. Strategies for Dealing with Difficult Customers and Managing Conflicts

Understanding the complexity of client interactions requires acknowledging that sometimes, we will face difficult customers or challenging circumstances. These settings are both a test and an opportunity to reveal your company's dedication to efficient customer service.

20.1. Identifying Difficult Customers

Difficult customers usually stand out due to certain behaviors such as aggressive demands, frequent escalations, or harsh criticisms. They may also be unsatisfied regardless of your efforts to meet their requirements. Discussing these distinctions helps customer service personnel approach each interaction strategically, leading to better outcomes.

20.2. Root Causes of Difficulty

Crucial to dealing with such customers is understanding the root cause of their difficult behavior. Most often, it's driven by unmet expectations, frustration with the product or service, incorrect use of products, or previous negative experiences with your company. In some cases, external factors like stress, personal problems, or cultural misunderstandings may influence a contentious interaction.

20.3. Patience is a Virtue

Patience and empathy are often your most valuable tools when dealing with difficult customers. Maintaining a calm demeanor and showing genuine concern for the customer's issues can de-escalate the situation and pave the way for trustworthy communication.

20.4. Active Listening

Active listening plays a crucial role in managing difficult customers. It helps to understand not just what customers are saying, but what they want or need. Repeating the customer's complaint or concern in your own words, asking for clarification, and acknowledging their feelings can showcase your dedication to solve the issue.

20.5. Appropriate Problem Solving

Once you've understood the customer's issue, appropriate problem-solving measures can be taken. This could be troubleshooting a product issue, offering a refund or replacement, or providing correct and clear information. If the solution isn't immediately apparent, engage with the customer to explore possible options.

20.6. Conflict Management Techniques

In conflict situations, adopting recognized techniques can improve outcomes. These include:

- Taking a break: Proposing a pause can help both parties calm down and think more clearly.

- Expressing understanding: Explicitly acknowledging the customer's frustration goes a long way towards resolution.

- Looking for the win-win scenario: Where possible, look for outcomes that satisfy both the customer's needs and your business goals.

20.7. When to Escalate and When to Let Go

Sometimes, despite your best efforts, the customer's issue may warrant escalation to a superior or different department. In rare cases, a customer may be so difficult or abusive that terminating business ties is the best course of action.

20.8. Training and Support for Staff

Managing difficult customers can be taxing on staff. Regular training and emotional support for your team are crucial to their wellbeing and preserving the quality of your customer service.

20.9. Learn and Improve

Each difficult situation should be seen as an opportunity to learn and improve your team's conflict management skills and overall customer service strategy. Regular debriefing with your team and recording key interactions helps in this process.

In sum, dealing with difficult customers is a delicate task requiring understanding, patience, communication skills, and problem-solving abilities. By mastering the art of turning difficult situations into opportunities for growth, you set your company up for the success it deserves. Strengthening your team's conflict management skills not only improves customer satisfaction but also makes your business a more fulfilling place to work, fostering a virtuous cycle of learning, development, and improvement. Embrace the challenge, and see your business reach newer heights.

Chapter 21. Advancing from Customer Satisfaction to Customer Delight

As a starting point for our exploration, it's incumbent upon us to understand the monumental shift taking place in the customer service landscape. Traditionally, businesses hustled to achieve a threshold called 'customer satisfaction.' But, in today's competitive market, this is no longer sufficient. We're witnessing a pivotal transition from 'customer satisfaction' to 'customer delight'. The leap is about fostering experiences that far exceed customer expectations, thus pushing their satisfaction meter to the point of elation or 'delight'.

21.1. Understanding Customer Delight

To create delightful experiences, it's imperative to first comprehend what 'customer delight' really signifies. The term refers to the process of exceeding customer expectations, by delivering superior service or product, and prompting a positive emotional reaction. Unlike customer satisfaction, which is largely met by fulfilling basic expectations, delight involves going several notches higher, adding unexpected value for the customer.

A delighted customer is likely to turn into a devoted brand advocate, highlighting the potential power of this transformative approach to customer service. Thus, investing in strategies to deliver customer delight isn't just about creating a transient 'wow' moment, it's about establishing a loyal customer base and ensuring sustainable business growth.

21.2. The Shift from Satisfaction to Delight

Customer satisfaction, though important, establishes a slightly complacent stance where a company merely aims to meet the standard requirements. The shift to customer delight, on the other hand, demands an anticipatory approach, which involves understanding and preemptively catering to customer needs even before they're vocalized.

There are several strategies to facilitate this transition:

1. *Proactive Communication*: Instead of waiting for the customer to state their needs, seek to anticipate them. Use communication channels to keep them informed and address potential concerns in advance.

2. *Delightful Details*: Pay attention to the details that add to the overall customer experience. It could be as simple as personalized recommendations or a thoughtful follow-up message expressing gratitude for their business.

3. *Prompt and Efficient Service*: Reduce customer effort and speed up resolution times. Efficiency is particularly valued in the service sector and can significantly tilt the scales towards delight.

21.3. Creating a Culture of Customer Delight

Cultivating an internal culture that supports and encourages efforts to delight customers is crucial. Without the staff understanding and owning this perspective, the execution could fall flat. Conduct regular training sessions, workshops, and discussions that emphasize the importance of going the extra mile for customer delight. Create a reward system that recognizes and applauds employees who successfully delight customers.

Embed this approach into your business policy and ensure it permeates all tiers of your organization. Maintain open communication channels within the company, creating a feedback loop to continually refine and improve your delight strategies.

21.4. Leveraging Technology for Delight

With the technology boom, businesses now have the tools to offer personalized experiences at scale. Employ data analytics to decipher customer preferences and anticipate needs. Predictive analytics, in particular, can help identify patterns and resolve issues even before they impact the customer.

Artificial Intelligence (AI) can be utilized for delivering precise solutions while reducing customer effort, enhancing the overall experience. Chatbots offer prompt assistance and 24/7 support, while CRM systems facilitate personalization by maintaining detailed customer profiles.

21.5. Measuring Customer Delight

Unlike satisfaction, delight isn't as straightforward to measure. It's qualitative, making it more challenging to track reliably through conventional metrics like surveys or scales. Innovative methods, such as the Net Promoter Score (NPS), serve to gauge the extent of customer delight. The NPS quantifies how likely a customer is to recommend your brand, which directly correlates with their level of delight. Other emotional analytics tools can also help measure customer sentiment post-interaction.

21.6. Piloting Challenges

Despite its many advantages, pursuing customer delight strategy is not without its challenges. Not all customers are alike, and personalizing experiences at scale can be daunting. Furthermore, going above and beyond may incur high costs without guaranteed returns. The key lies in striking a balance that delights customers without compromising the business's resources.

In conclusion, the passage from customer satisfaction to delight is an evolutionary journey that demands foresight, planning, and efficient use of technology. However, the rewards in terms of customer loyalty, increased advocacy, and the resulting business growth make it an endeavour worth undertaking.

Chapter 22. Leveraging Technology for Enhanced Customer Communications

Technology has rapidly expanded and evolved over the past several decades, revolutionizing the way businesses operate and communicate with their customers. By leveraging the power of technology, companies have managed to improve communication processes, offering faster response times, personalized interactions, and swift problem resolution. Equipping your organization with the most effective technologies can significantly boost customer satisfaction levels, leading to increased loyalty and business growth.

22.1. Understanding Your Customer Communication Channels

As the foundational step, it's crucial to understand the various means of communication your business currently employs. Traditional modes might include phone services, in-person, or written correspondences. With technology, the spectrum of channels expands to include emails, social media, live chat, and even AI-powered tools like chatbots.

By mapping out these channels, you can begin to discern where technology can be best integrated to offer smoother, faster, and more effective communication. Identify gaps in your current system — Are there long waiting times? Are some queries left unresolved? These are areas where technology can be applied to improve overall customer experience.

22.2. Harnessing the Power of Social Media

In modern society, social media plays a powerful role in customer communication. Platforms such as Facebook, Twitter, Instagram, and LinkedIn offer unrivaled opportunities to connect with your customer base. They enable businesses to handle inquiries effectively, resolve issues timely, and engage customers with dynamic content.

Automation features, such as scheduled posts and automated responses, can be employed to manage your social media interactions efficiently. Social listening tools are highly beneficial too, allowing you to gauge customer sentiment and understand your brand's online reputation.

22.3. Integrating Live Chat and Chatbots

Live chat is another customer communication tool that's gaining popularity due to its immediacy and efficiency. It's an incredible technology that allows real-time conversations between customers and customer service representatives.

For further efficiency and 24/7 service, chatbots or virtual assistants can be integrated. These AI-powered tools can handle simple queries, guide customers through standard processes, and escalate more complex issues to human agents. While retaining the personal touch is important, the integration of AI in such areas can reduce response times and ease the workload on your customer service team.

22.4. Efficient Email Automation

Email remains a popular communication channel, offering direct and substantive correspondence with customers. Automated email responses can confirm that a customer's query has been received and is being processed. Also, setting up automated sequences for frequently asked questions or regular updates can help in managing customer inquiries effectively while saving time.

22.5. Leveraging CRM Tools

Customer Relationship Management (CRM) tools have been a game-changer in the realm of customer service. These technological systems organize information about customers, facilitating an understanding of their preferences, purchase history, and past interactions with your company.

Using a CRM system, your team can deliver personalized service, provide relevant offers, and foresee potential issues even before they arise. Furthermore, integration of CRM systems with other communication channels can provide a cohesive view of customer interactions, helping your team deliver unified and efficient service.

22.6. Implementing Self-Service Options

Self-service technology empowers customers to resolve their queries independently by giving them direct access to information. FAQ pages, instructional how-to videos, and community forums allow customers to find the solutions they need swiftly.

Interactive Voice Response (IVR) systems can also act as a form of self-service, allowing customers to navigate through automated phone menus to find the assistance they require. This way customers can resolve simple queries immediately, leaving your team available to handle more complex issues.

22.7. Harnessing Big Data for Customer Insights

In today's business landscape, data drives decisions. Collecting, processing, and analyzing customer interaction data can provide invaluable insights into customer behavior and preferences. This intelligence can inform changes in customer service strategy, helping predict customer needs and potential pain-points. By providing proactive service, you improve customer satisfaction, retain more clients, and foster strong customer relationships.

The infusion of technology into business communication processes has sparked remarkable enhancements in customer service. Adopting and integrating these technologies can transform the way you connect with your customers, leading to heightened satisfaction and loyalty. Remember, the journey towards enhanced customer service does not stop with the implementation of technology. Regularly update, analyze, and tweak your systems and strategies to keep offering state-of-the-art service. Before long your organization will be recognized for its excellence in customer communication. Mastering the art of leveraging technology for customer communication is not just desirable, it is indispensable.

Chapter 23. Measuring Outcomes: Tools to Assess and Improve Customer Service Excellence

Monitoring, assessing, and improving customer service is not only integral but indeed the lifeblood of any organization seeking to deliver unmatched customer experiences. Let's delve deep into the tools that can assist organizations in assessing and subsequently improving their Customer Service Excellence.

23.1. Understanding the Need for Measuring Outcomes

Before discussing the specific tools and methods used to measure customer service excellence, it's beneficial to understand why it is essential. The primary goal of customer service is to ensure customer satisfaction, maximize customer retention, and enhance brand reputation. Organizations often grapple with clarifying the impacts of their customer service strategies. Here, measurement tools become the cornerstone. These tools not only serve as mechanisms for evaluating effectiveness but also provide insights to optimize resources, fine-tune approaches, and pinpoint areas of improvement—ultimately steering organizations towards operational excellence and unparalleled customer satisfaction.

23.2. Quantitative Tools

Quantitative tools help in collecting standardized data that can be statistically analyzed. These tools lean more towards the 'hard' side of metrics, focusing on numerical outcomes derived from customer interactions.

1. Customer Satisfaction Score (CSAT) CSAT is a straightforward tool used to assess the customer's immediate level of satisfaction with a product, service, or particular interaction. Customers are usually asked to rate their satisfaction on a numerical scale.

2. Net Promoter Score (NPS) NPS measures customer loyalty by asking a single question, "On a scale of 0 to 10, how likely are you to recommend this product/service/company to a friend or colleague?" Companies use NPS scores to anticipate growth and customer retention.

3. First Contact Resolution (FCR) FCR tracks whether a customer's issue is resolved in their first interaction with a support agent. A high FCR indicates that the company's customer service team is competent and efficient, leading to satisfied customers.

23.3. Qualitative Tools

Alongside these quantitative measures, employing qualitative tools is equally crucial. Such tools provide insights into customer perceptions, expectations, and experiences—delivering a more holistic view of the customer journey.

1. Customer Feedback One of the simplest yet most powerful tools, customer feedback, in the form of reviews or comments, provides firsthand insights into what customers think about a company's product or service.

2. Customer Interviews One-on-one customer interviews allow for in-depth conversation and understanding, revealing intricacies about customer expectations, perceptions, and experiences that surveys may miss.

3. Social Media Monitoring Listening to what customers are saying on social media platforms helps businesses gain direct access to

customer opinions, concerns, and suggestions.

23.4. Leveraging Technological Tools

The digital era has brought forth a plethora of technology-based tools that have revolutionized the customer service landscape. These tools create opportunities to automate processes, increase efficiency, and most importantly, improve customer relationships.

1. Customer Relationship Management (CRM) Systems Essential for any modern customer service operation, CRM systems centralize customer interactions, facilitating team collaboration and effective customer service.

2. Customer Service Software Specialized customer service software, such as help-desk solutions or ticketing systems, aid in tracking, prioritizing, and solving customer support tickets swiftly—an essential factor in today's fast-paced, high-expectation customer landscape.

3. Artificial Intelligence (AI) and Chatbots AI plays a crucial role in automating repetitive tasks and providing instantaneous responses to customer enquiries. Chatbots, powered by AI, can effectively handle a large volume of customer interactions with consistent, swift service.

23.5. Combining Tools for Comprehensive Metrics

In the bid to deliver excellent customer service, utilizing a blend of quantitative, qualitative, and technological tools plays a decisive role. Companies must posture themselves to embrace this mix to leverage customer data holistically, ensuring they deliver service that not only satisfies customers but also turns them into dedicated brand advocates.

Investing in potent customer service insights enhances every aspect of an organization's operations. It paves the way for building robust relationships with customers and enables the team to focus on areas worth leveraging and improving. These tools are your tactical arsenal to navigate the customer service battlefield, turning challenges into opportunities to delight customers, solicit loyalty, and, ultimately, secure your brand's triumphant success in the marketplace. Now, armed with these strategies, you're ready to march towards measurable, impactful outcomes. Happy measuring!

www.ingramcontent.com/pod-product-compliance
Lightning Source LLC
Chambersburg PA
CBHW062258290526
45794CB00006B/2602